Ambassador

Speaking to the Nations
by
David K. Ewen, M.Ed.

Silver Anniversary Series

ISBN-13: 978-1725199972

ISBN-10: 1725199971

About the Book

The book Ambassador talks about the authors role and responsibilities as a field Ambassador in the area of education. Readers will understand the personality and behaviors necessary for such a position. It is interesting to note that the international responsibility of a field Ambassador is strictly civilian in nature. This is a look at how civilians stand on the global stage and speak to the nation's as a field ambassador. The book is written in narrative form as in a lecture.

.

David K. Ewen, M.Ed.

About the Author

David K. Ewen, M.Ed. is an author, speaker, and publisher. He has been in the field of Education since 1988 and added on the experiences of book publishing since 1994 and has been deeply in media production, marketing, and distribution since then. As a public speaker, David K. Ewen, M.Ed. first reached the six New England states promoting the self-publishing independent press industry in 1998 while serving as Executive Director of the New England Publishers Association. This speaking tour was complimented by a weekly hour-long radio broadcast talk show hosted on WORC 1310 AM and WGFP 940 AM. The show author of the week was spun off into a short-lived weekly television show broadcasted from the CAT studios in Westborough Massachusetts. David has been deeply involved in multimedia production and distribution since 1998. David K. Ewen, M.Ed. held a second speaking tour that lasted 11 years touring the seven states of New York

and New England at 52 venues lecturing on 18 different topics. This was called the "Professor Lecture Series" running from 2004 to 2015 with the flagship lecture "Publish Your Book Guaranteed" Shortly following the conclusion of the professor lecture series tour, David K. Ewen, M.Ed. went out on the global stage to speak to the nations for the purposes of training and education. As a civilian field Ambassador in education, his initial outreach was in Japan, China, Vietnam, Saudi Arabia, and Russia. David holds a faculty position at the American Academy in Beijing, China. Today, when David is working on the global stage speaking to the nations he reaches out to the civilian community in Asia, the Middle East, and Europe. The technical background of David K. Ewen, M.Ed. comes from his initial work as a quality assurance specialist and senior analyst programmer in the 1980s and 1990s. His undergraduate work at the University of Massachusetts focused on mathematics with a minor in computer science. His post-graduate focused on education with a minor in management earning him a master's degree in education in 1988 (M.Ed., Cambridge College). The business experience of David K. Ewen, M.Ed. comes from the founding of Ewen Prime Company in 1994. The experience was demonstrated during his 11-year tour in the seven states of New York and New England with the lecture, "Building and Maintaining a Profitable Consulting Practice". This was part of the "Professor Lecture Series" tour.

Ambassador

When I tell people that I am an ambassador what I really mean is that I am a field in ambassador in the field of education. Many countries around the world look to the United States for their educational needs.

Many years ago, the founder of Microsoft Bill Gates had provided an infusion of investment into the educational needs of Vietnam to help develop TOPICA Edtech Group. This was in 2006. Eleven years later, I served as a faculty member to develop international communication needs of entrepreneurs, community leaders, industry experts, government officials, and others.

In 2017, I work with a Russian school to develop their online education program in entrepreneurial studies and International Communication. This was a year-long project.

My start on the global stage speaking to the nation's begin in 2012 as a copywriter in India to support services that were delivered to Canada, the United Kingdom, Australia, and the United States. My first lectures where in 2014 for NTT Learning Systems in Japan. This was later followed with a faculty position which later turned into the position of Dean of Teachers at Dr. Lan Academy located in Shanghai, China. As time went on, my voice on the global stage reaching the nations covered the territories of Asia, the Middle East, Europe, and South America.

The benefit of working with different cultures is that I can find the common denominator among all nations to bridge the gap causing conflict and misunderstanding. It is a joy to see that humankind is a people of one kind in different nations with different cultures. Yet, we are all the same when it comes down to how we care about families, work in our careers, put Focus to education, and have a hope for our future. In this way we are all the same.

The truth about my first experience related to any kind of international concept was when I met my wife (from Medellin, Colombia) in March of 2002. At the time she was an illegal alien who did not speak my native language nor did I speak hers. What is significant about the date that we met is that it was 6 months after the tragedies that occurred on September 11th 2001. The United States was still recovering from the wounds of terrorism and the Department of Homeland Security had yet to be established.

Over the next several years, immigration law with all of its requirements would be changing frequently as it adapted to a new Global understanding of immigration. It took 6 years for my wife to become a United States citizen and be able to vote in American presidential elections. She has even satisfied the duty of jury duty as all United States citizens do. The process was daunting especially with all that was going on in the years that followed the 9-11 tragedy.

I look back at the process of my wife becoming a citizen. I remember standing in line outside the JFK government building in Boston waiting for the doors to open. It was raining that day while I was holding my wife to keep her dry. I use this example as a demonstration of knowing what it truly is like to go through the immigration and naturalization process in America. Just the simple statement of standing in the rain says it all. This is one example out of many.

I did not know that my experience with my wife to become naturalized and for her to go to school to learn my native language would play a significant impact on my role as a field ambassador in education speaking on the global stage to the nations. It seems that it would have been necessary to have that first-hand obscene what it is like to be outside of the United States looking in. I felt that way when I was standing in the rain. The paperwork and the difficult interviews and the long drive into Boston where frequent.

Fast forward to the year 2014, when I first started speaking two professional industry experts and government officials in Japan, I understood how they perceived me and how they were not aware of my experience. In time they did become aware of my experience and I noticed a huge appreciation which helped bridge the gap that causes misunderstanding and false perceptions. I understood their goals and desires. It was all because I stood in the rain and more.

As a Field Ambassador, I used the field of Education serving as a civilian to reach other civilians in other nations. By satisfying their need for an American style education in the areas of international communication and entrepreneurial studies, I was able to recognize various political and religious perceptions that serve as a repellent between cultures. In a gentle way, I found ways to rebuke that repellent that bridged the gap caused by misunderstanding and other false perceptions.

The experience of being a Field Ambassador created a storage of knowledge that's when used properly created wisdom. It is that wisdom that I rely on today as I stand on the global stage speaking to the nations representing the United States.

My lectures here in the United States are not the same as when I speak two others on foreign territory. People from other nations look at a field ambassador in a different way then a university professor from their native land. The words I use and the behaviors I show are being very closely observed when I speak to my international guests online.

To enhance the experience of being on the global stage speaking to the nations, it is necessary to offer a best-in-class service held at the highest level. The technology includes a broadcast capability with high-def cameras, visual graphics for logos, and special effects green screen background (Chromakey) as seen in the movies. This provides an augmented virtual reality giving a professional appearance while I am in front of my international audience.

A professional image as well as behavioral responses with properly chosen words has significant importance. There is no second chance to make that very critical first impression. After that first impression, it is important to maintain a high expectation that exudes trustworthiness, amicability, and a sense of authority.

I mentioned that the first impression must include a sense of authority. What I meant by that is to generate and earned respect. Not a demanded respect, but in earned respect. The sense of authority produces a feeling of confidence and self-awareness witch in turn generates trustworthiness. The trustworthiness in time creates and environment that is amicable and open. Given all of those, education can be performed offering the important services of international communication and entrepreneurial studies.

The notion of respect and Authority as previously mentioned is used to create the bridge that reaches over the gap of misunderstanding and false perceptions. This is a leadership quality used internationally by anyone in any type of ambassador capacity. My role as a field ambassador with an educational focus is civilian in nature and puts attention to international communication and entrepreneurial studies.

It is my opinion that the role of a field ambassador is not one that a person can be formally trained for. My experience has shown that situations that our lives through an extended period of time is what prepares one to become a field ambassador. It was in 1988 that I and in education after earning my master's degree in education (M.Ed.). In 1994, leadership skills were developed when I launched my Publishing Company play dark evolved into the New England Publishers

Association of which I served as executive director. Public speaking was developed since 1998 with part-time it is in broadcast radio and television. The Professor Lecture Series was an 11-year tour 52 venues in the seven states of New York and New England. All this and more, produce the skills of fast prudent decision-making resulting in predictable logical outcomes. These skills are critical. We live in a fast-moving world. Evolving technology is making the world move even faster. Decisions must be fast and done with authoritative confidence.

I've just spoken about the skills necessary for a field ambassador. The personality and behavior of such a person it's not common across all civilians. This is not to demean those who are not field ambassadors. What is being illustrated here is a significant character that is required for a field ambassador to be effective due to the variety of cultures, religions, and political beliefs. Those that follow the instruction, tutorage, or Revelation provided by a field ambassador have extremely high expectations that go beyond differences in religion, politics, in cultures. A field ambassador do not be afraid of the expectation that they are held to. I have often said, that for this reason, a field ambassador is not a job; it is a responsibility. Do not think of a field ambassador as a career or vocation. It is a responsibility. Granted that's how they are paid as if it was a job, but it is not the kind of job that you clock in and clock out. There are no vacations to speak of.

As you can see, the challenges of a field ambassador hold responsibilities that go beyond a traditional career among civilians. Keep in mind that the field Ambassador is a civilian position. In my case, the field I have chosen is education. There are other fields that civilian ambassadors evolve into overtime through experience to create knowledge which is used to produce wisdom.

The responsibilities of a field ambassador is conducted through love and passion for what the calling is. The rigorous schedule and requirements are simply overcome by the love and passion of taking ownership of the responsibilities of a field ambassador.

I did not ask to be a field ambassador. It just happened. That is true with other field ambassadors. An opportunity arises and there is a need to fill and given the right person, a field ambassador is born into a responsibility that they had not foreseen or planned for. Never in my wildest dreams would I think that I would be married to an illegal alien (now a US citizen) and later become a field ambassador on the global stage speaking to the nations. I became an ambassador not by choice.

In my early days as a field ambassador, I thought about what the best characteristics and behaviors would be necessary. The book of Galatians in the Bible chapter 5 verse 22 through 23 talks about the fruits of the spirit. Those I consider part of the personality that is necessary for an effective trustworthy field ambassador. The Bible also has scripture in the book of Jeremiah chapter 29 verse 11 that talks about God's plan each and everyone of us. I believe that my role as a field Ambassador was part of God's plan that I must be obedient to and apply the personality traits of the fruits of the spirit as shown in the book of Galatians.

Galatians 5:22-23 (NIV) But the fruit of the Spirit is love, joy, peace, forbearance, kindness, goodness, faithfulness, gentleness and self-control. Against such things there is no law.

I use the book of Galatians to help me determine the proper personality traits necessary for a field ambassador. The personality traits is one thing that is internal, but the actions are external in are the behaviors. So I must look at not only personality but also behaviors. I can better understand the definition of a field Ambassador when I look at personality and behavior as separate entities. The personality is in the mind and the behavior is the action that is visible.

It took a long time to develop the behavior traits for a field ambassador to recognize and follow. It was developed and released in the year 2017. This was part of the development of the Boston Institute of Business Leaders and Entrepreneurs. We call it the Seven Pillars for the Models of Excellence. The Seven Pillars representing the Models of Excellence are motivation, organization, discipline, ethics, learning, and strength to endure. The 7th pillar is a compass of the previous six. More will be explained later.

A field Ambassador can be effective when they study the n fruits of the spirit in the book of Galatians and the Seven Pillars for the Models of Excellence. The fruits of the spirit represent personality and the Models of Excellence represent behavior. The combined personality and behavior is what defines an effective field ambassador. It is a lifelong I'm going learning process to become better at the traits associated with personality and behavior. The role of a field ambassador is a journey and the destination is ongoing.

The effective development of a field ambassador's personality and behavior is what will generate respect from other nations. Respect is something that is earned and not given. That being said, where can effort is needed to develop proper personality and behavior to create a field Ambassador that is respected on the global stage speaking to the nations.

<u>RESPECT</u>

There are so many ways to describe what respect is such as the song from Urethra Franklin released in 1967. My take on the word respect is not so much the meaning but more importantly the feeling that it evokes. There is a feeling when giving respect and a feeling when receiving respect. The desirable feelings for both giving and receiving respect requires a mentality of understanding.

A good way to define what respect is can be done by demonstrating what it isn't and that is called disrespect. Examples of disrespect is intentional deception, manipulation, and selfish behavior. I talked about this in my book Discerning Evil. I will explore that and more here.

A young person considers the word respect applying to behavior toward their elders. A person with more years has experience. That experience comes from the investment of time and what was done during that time. Some of the things that were done consists of mistakes. Those mistakes are called investment in experience. What do you have after you invest in experience? You have wisdom. Wisdom is knowing what to do with the investment of experience which relates to knowledge. It is the wisdom that an older person has which has the authority of making wise decisions. People with wisdom are more likely to make decisions resulting in an easy conclusion that is more efficient. Without wisdom, decisions come, and the result may not be so efficient.

At the Boston Institute of Business Leaders and Entrepreneurs, we have developed and released the Seven Pillars for the Models of Excellence that represent a model for wisdom. This includes motivation, organization, discipline, ethics (knowing what is right and wrong), learning, strength (long lasting endurance to not give up), and a combination of those already mentioned. For example, organization and discipline are paired nicely together. Motivation in learning are also paired nicely together.

The Seven Pillars who are the Models of Excellence offer an opportunity to invest in experience more quickly to achieve the knowledge that is applied to wisdom. The keywords are experience, knowledge, wisdom. The experience in life is what gives a person knowledge.

Knowledge then becomes all that would a person knows. Wisdom is being able to use that knowledge effectively. There must be enough knowledge so that the resources are in place so that wisdom can be applied. The development of that knowledge comes over time which is why an elder person is known to have wisdom. An elder person has the experience over time that generates knowledge which a pool of resources exercise by wisdom.

Along with wisdom comes to behavior which makes wisdom recognize. This is why the Seven Pillars for the models of Excellence include such behaviors as motivation. Motivation requires a sense of maturity that goes above and beyond laziness. There is a sense of responsibility and being held accountable for our actions. This kind of behavior evokes a sense of wisdom. The observance of wisdom is by way of action which is behavioral in a responsible and ethical way and applies knowledge efficiently.

The behaviors of ethics and motivation together have the meaning of doing the right thing and wanting to do the right thing. The behaviors of discipline and learning have the meaning of being focused to evolve to a more improved level. The behaviors of organization and the strength to never give up have the meaning of being patient and take it one step at a time toward the right direction with a plan. These are three examples of how the behaviors of the Seven Pillars of the Models of Excellence can be put forth to applying wisdom.

The actions associated with the Seven Pillars of the models of Excellence are the result of the behaviors that it forced it. When applying and behaving with motivation, organization, discipline, ethics, learning, and the strength of endurance the manifestation of these behaviors will be observable and measurable.

Given that the exercising of the Seven Pillars of the models of Excellence are observable and measurable that in turn develops wisdom, one can see that there is power in the results. This is why wisdom has authority. In many cultures, the elderly is highly respected because their wisdom has Authority. In other cultures, the wisdom is not respected because it is a culture of slumber and disrespect.

There is the understanding that respect is something that is earned and not given. That is true. That is why the Seven Pillars of the Models of Excellence explain a behavior that is proper that intern earns respect. It makes sense that behaviors that include motivation, organization, discipline, ethics, learning, and the strength to endure, would be observed as something to respect.

Even people with earned respect do not receive the respect they deserve. Those that infringe upon respect and cause disrespect fall into one of three categories. They might be jealous of a person who is respected. They might be afraid of a person who is respected. They might be intimidated of a person who is respected. Jealousy, fear, and intimidation are the behaviors that are the root of disrespect. Sprouting from the root of disrespect is deception, manipulation, and selfish behavior. This means jealousy, fear, and intimidation is the cause of deception, manipulation, and selfish behavior.

Disrespect is easy to discern and recognize by observing the immediate behaviors of jealousy, fear, and intimidation that result in the actions of deception, manipulation, and selfish behavior. By confronting the behaviors and the actions of disrespect, one can begin to stomp out disrespect.

If disrespect is stomped out, then more positive results can replace putting forth respect. The behaviors and actions of disrespect can be replaced with the Seven Pillars of the Models of Excellence which include motivation, organization, discipline, ethics, learning, strength to endure, and a combination of the others.

In the Bible in the book of Galatians chapter 5 verse 22 through 23, the scripture reads, but the fruit of the spirit is love, joy, peace, forbearance, kindness, goodness, faithfulness, gentleness and self-control. Against such things there is no law. (NIV version). The King James version of the same scripture reads but the fruit of the spirit is love, joy, peace, long-suffering, gentleness, goodness, faith, meekness, temperance: against such there is no law.

The fruits of the spirit in the book of Galatians describe a behavior in the form of personality traits. Without the personality traits, the behavior could not be recognized. It is important that personality is what defines good and bad. The fruits of the spirit is what defines what is good. The subsequent resource the Seven Pillars the Models of Excellence stand on the foundation of the fruits of the spirit because the personality is necessary before the behavior can be seen. An example is when a person speaks comes first from what is in their mind. The speaking is the action and what is in a person's mind is the personality. Thus the nature of the language a person uses can help others discern what their personality is like.

We are learning here that the earning of respect comes from behaviors that are supported by the foundation of personality. The personality has been defined as the fruits of the spirit as shown in the book of Galatians. The behavior has been defined as what comes from the Seven Pillars the Models of Excellence. All of this is developed over time through experience. Therefore, the investment in experience produces knowledge. Wisdom is knowing how to use that knowledge. Given sufficient knowledge wisdom is naturally born.

The passage of time develops wisdom through the accumulation of knowledge built with experience that includes rewards and consequences. Rewards encourage behavior. Consequences discourages behavior. In the beginning a reward will create a bad behavior that later will be corrected with a consequence in the future. By default, the bad behavior is discouraged beat it with a reward or a consequence. A temporary reward such as a casino winning will suffer from consequences of ongoing gambling. A temporary reward such as a good feeling from smoking will suffer from consequences of failed health. The bad behavior does not win. It never does.

There are two ways to learn something. The easy way and the hard way. The hard way is through consequences of bad behavior which never wins. The easy way is to develop a personality that relates to the fruits of the spirit as shown in the book of Galatians Chapter 5 Verse 22 through 23. That personality serves as the foundation of the behavior shown in the Seven Pillars of the Models of Excellence.

There are those who choose not to be guided such as what is written in the

Bible to describe proper personality which can in turn service as the foundation of the Seven Pillars of the Models of Excellence. Ignorance is what pushes people to suffer consequences to the extent that they finally end up in jail starting to read the Bible. Look it up online. It's easy to find examples of ex-convicts who found Jesus in jail. The consequences were great in numbers and intensity. This is an example of hitting rock bottom which means the discovery of learning through consequences may not be the best thing.

If you have not hit rock bottom, then attending a bible-based church and understanding the fruits of the spirit as shown in the book of Galatians chapter 5 verses 22 through 23 is an extremely powerful start. This could help change personality traits leading toward improve behavior. The new Behavior could be supported on the foundation of the Seven Pillars of the Models of Excellence. If determined to put those two together, the guidance toward a better life with respect can easily be a achieved.

As we return to our topic of respect, let's talk about how one should receive it. As said before, respect is earned and not given. That being said, respect should not be expected. Instead what should be expected is focusing on the fruits of the spirit to support personality traits that can build the behaviors as shown in the Seven Pillars of the Models of Excellence. The behaviors of motivation, organization, discipline, ethics, learning, and the strength to endure will naturally earn respect because it is what other people can observe.

The nature of respect is to be followed. People like to follow respect. That means the earned respect must be valid for it to be genuinely long-lasting. It's not easy to achieve. But it is so much better than the alternative. The investment in experience to get knowledge that serves as the foundation of wisdom is what earns respect. It is not done overnight. It is a journey. developing the fruits of the spirit as shown in Galatians chapter 5 Verse 22 through 23 is a lifelong journey. But the scripture gives the guidance as to what that lifelong journey should be. During that Journey, the personality traits being developed serve as the foundation of behavior seen in the Seven Pillars Models of Excellence.

Start your journey today. Attend a weekly based church. Fellowship with other church members so that you are not alone. The journey was never intended to be done. Work on improving yourself. As a guide, use the Seven Pillars the models of Excellence as a foundation to the behaviors that are respected. During your journey, you will see the reward of respect. Don't give up. Keep going. The Bible shows the way with the guidance of the proper spiritual leaders of a bible-based congregation. It may be a different life than what you had before, but it will be a life of less consequences and more rewards. At first, this lifestyle will seem strange and unusual. When living a life of consequences for so long, of course it would because you would be on new path that has true biblical guidance. There's nothing to lose and a lot to gain.

It's worth it. It's in your favor to develop wisdom that earns respect. It also makes your life easier. Take advantage of it. Be encouraged by not being alone. That is what the church is for. People fail when they're alone because they don't have the help and encouragement.

I give thanks to my church family so that I have the guidance and encouragement. I thank God for giving me a more structured path toward wisdom that earns respect. The respect on talking about is not one of pride. A prideful Behavior to does not respect.

Fondest wishes go to you and your loved ones. I pray that the words in the Bible give guidance for a better personality that produces behavior that offer less concert inboard rewards in your life.   My hope is the Seven Pillars of the Models of Excellence provide a strong Foundation to behavior that produces positive actions in your life.

<u>Seven Pillars of the Models of Excellence</u>

The seven pillars of the Models of Excellence include motivation, organization, discipline, ethics, learning, strength, and combinations of the previous six pillars. The Models of Excellence is the engine providing a mechanism of growth to five countries supported by the Educational Outreach Ambassadorship (O.E.A.). The E.O.A. is a moniker used to represent and outreach to Japan, China, Vietnam, Saudi Arabia, and Russia.

What is shared here in this content has also been shared around the world with people and prominent position such as an astronaut who landed on the moon, an athlete training for the Olympics, government officials and dignitaries, and others in high level positions responsible for impacts on global issues.

The value of what you will learn here has been realized by others around the world looking to understand their purpose and how to fulfill it in a way that leaves a legacy that can be shared by others for edification.

There are seven pillars representing the Models of Excellence. They are the following:

(1) Motivation
(2) Organization
(3) Discipline
(4) Ethics
(5) Learning
(6) Strength
(7) Combination

The seventh pillar, "Combination" is a combination of the previous six pillars. Each can stand alone and combined with others.

<u>Motivation</u>

The first pillar called motivation is the get up and go attitude that is self-driven offering a reason for acting and behaving in a beneficial way. Motivation is void of a state of Slumber and laziness.

It is easy to be in a state of slumber and behave in a lazy way. It requires fortitude and perseverance to be motivated. This requires a desired focused attention to be void of a lazy behavior. This action is self-driven and not controlled or swayed by others. Motivation is a responsibility that is based on action.

We all have choices in life. The choice to accept and embrace motivation is ours alone. We can choose to accept it or deny it. Accepting it has rewards. Denying it has consequences. The choice determines the outcome of rewards or consequences.

In Proverbs 6:9 the scripture reads, "How long will you slumber, O sluggard? When will you rise from your sleep?

<u>Organization</u>

Having organization put structure in life so that there is a path toward an objective allowing for the reward of a goal to be achieved. Without organization, there is no road map to a goal because no goal exists. Those who have organization accomplish things that are beneficial to themselves and others. Without organization. There is miss-direction and a sense of unawareness. The result is a confusing state of mind. By having organization, there is understanding, assured behavior, incompetent awareness. This allows accomplishments and goals to be achieved.

In 1st Corinthians 14:40, the scripture reads, "Let all things be done decently and in order."

In Luke 14:28, the scripture reads, "For which of you, intending to build a tower, does not sit down first and count the cost, whether he has enough to finish it"

<u>Discipline</u>

Discipline is knowing the difference between what you must do compared to what you want to do. Sometimes what you want to do interferes with what you must do. Doing what you must do will never negatively impact what you want to do. Discipline is understanding priorities in life by recognizing what must be done. There is an understanding of consequences when priorities are not met. That understanding insurance that consequences are avoided resulting in priorities taking precedence in our lives. Discipline requires obedience to the focused attention of the priorities that must be done. It involves a constant awareness and action to fulfill priorities as necessary.

In Hebrews 12:11, the scripture reads, "Now no chastening seems to be joyful for the present, but painful; nevertheless, afterward it yields the peaceable fruit of righteousness to those who have been trained by it."

In Titus 1:8, the scripture reads, "but hospitable, a lover of what is good, sober-minded, just, holy, self-controlled,"

<u>Ethics</u>

Ethics is knowing the difference between right and wrong. By not having ethics, ron can be committed without being aware that it is not right. There is a firm division between what is considered right and what is considered wrong. One way that is created is by the legal system. A more important way is what is inherently understood and expected within Humanity. The actions of people, when honorable and respectful, tend to lean toward what is right and steer away from what is wrong.

In Luke 6:31, the scripture reads, "And just as you want men to do to you, you also do to them likewise."

In Matthew 7:12, the scripture reads, "Therefore, whatever you want men to do to you, do also to them, for this is the Law and the Prophets."

<u>Learning</u>

The process of learning never ends and we can all receive edification from others. By being mindful and respectful to the understanding that learning never ends we can achieve greater wisdom beyond the knowledge of which it is founded. Education not only comes from schools, but also from experiences, conversation, suffering through consequences, achieving successes, and sharing with others. There are so many avenues of learning and edification that an open mind can receive and continue to grow beyond expectations and to greater awareness.

In Proverbs 1:5 the scripture reads, "A wise man will hear and increase learning, And a man of understanding will attain wise counsel,"

In Luke 6:40, the scripture reads, "A disciple is not above his teacher, but everyone who is perfectly trained will be like his teacher."

<u>Strength</u>

Strength represents not giving up. It is the endurance to continue even when difficult times are ahead. With strength, the adversities in life will not be a hindrance to reaching goals and becoming successful. Being void of strength allows any obstacle to prevent moving forward to any success resulting in total absolute failure. To avoid failure, strength is necessary to endure and overcome obstacles put in our path. Strength is also represented by self-control to persevere and continue forth through storms in life. When considering strength needed in life consider the words endurance and self-control.

In Colossians 1:11, the scripture reads, "strengthened with all might, according to His glorious power, for all patience and longsuffering with joy;"

In Philippians 4:13, the scripture reads, "I can do all things through Christ who strengthens me."

Combination

The seventh and final pillar representing models of Excellence is a combination of the previous six. For example to be organized you must be disciplined. To have ethics you must learn what is right and wrong. To have motivation you must have strength

One of the reasons there are seven pillars representing the models of Excellence is that the number 7 has significance. In the Book of Genesis, God created the heavens and the Earth and rested on the 7th Day. The number 7 represent something being finished or complete. Thereafter, in the Bible, the number 7 represented define perfection or completion.

In no way does the Seven Pillars representing the models of Excellence replace or make less of the nine fruits of the spirit as noted in the book of Galatians. In Galatians 5:22-23, the scripture reads, "But the fruit of the Spirit is love, joy, peace, longsuffering, kindness, goodness, faithfulness, gentleness, self-control. Against such there is no law."

<u>Discerning Evil</u>

To maintain models of excellence in our lives there must be a minimal level of distraction. The ability to discern evil ensures that's our wrongness found in the world we live in does not deter us from the direction necessary for us to succeed. The evil to be discerned are in the categories of deception, manipulation, and selfishness by others who may make effort to influence us. The recognition of this evil in advance will easily stomp out a possible deception, manipulation, and selfishness that others try to impose upon us.

In 1st John 4:1-3, the scripture reads, "Beloved, do not believe every spirit, but test the spirits to see whether they are from God, for many false prophets have gone out into the world. By this you know the Spirit of God: every spirit that confesses that Jesus Christ has come in the flesh is from God, and every spirit that does not confess Jesus is not from God. This is the spirit of the antichrist, which you heard was coming and now is in the world already."

<u>Deception</u>

In the bible from the book of Proverbs chapter 6 verses 16 to 19 says "There are six things that the Lord hates, seven that are an abomination to him: haughty eyes, a lying tongue, and hands that shed innocent blood, a heart that devises wicked plans, feet that make haste to run to evil, a false witness who breathes out lies, and one who sows discord among brothers. "

In the bible from the book of Revelations chapter 12 verse 9 says "And the great dragon was thrown down, that ancient serpent, who is called the devil and Satan, the deceiver of the whole world— he was thrown down to the earth, and his angels were thrown down with him."

In the bible from the book of first of Timothy chapter 4 verse 1, the scripture reads: Now the Spirit expressly says that in later times some will depart from the faith by devoting themselves to deceitful spirits and teachings of demons,

Different evil behavior is defined as one or more of the characteristics of deception, manipulation, or operating under self-serving behavior. Self-serving behavior is selfishness.

Let us talk about deception and define what it is. Deception is the action of deceiving someone. It is action that results in deceit. Deception is fraudulent behavior involving trickery, chicanery, slyness. A bluff to give pretense of something else is a form of treachery. This deception has many purposes including manipulation and to satisfy selfishness. Manipulation and selfishness encompass two of the tree axis of evil. Deception is the third. manipulation and selfishness can result from deception. This example shows how deception, manipulation, and selfishness operate together.

The act of deception has the intent of not telling the truth. The truth is hidden. God says that the truth will set you free. With deception, there is no freedom. The difficulty from continual deception has to do with keeping the story straight for long term believability. If the story resulting from deception has no truth, the difficulty of maintaining consistency has difficulties. Fabricating a story with the intent of swaying a person's belief's or actions require continual fabrication to ensure successful deception. The person of deceit does not know how far they must act on deceiving. This behavior fails in the long term, because the discernment of fake behavior cannot last forever.

<u>Manipulation</u>

In the bible from the book of Matthew chapter 7 verse 15, the scripture reads: "Beware of false prophets, who come to you in sheep's clothing but inwardly are ravenous wolves.

In the bible in the book of Matthew chapter 24 verse 4, the scripture reads: And Jesus answered them, "See that no one leads you astray.

In the bible in the book of Hebrews chapter 13 verse 8 to 9, the scripture reads: Jesus Christ is the same yesterday and today and forever. Do not be led away by diverse and strange teachings, for it is good for the heart to be strengthened by grace, not by foods, which have not benefited those devoted to them.

Manipulation involves the skillful handing or controlling something or someone. The purpose of that skillful handling may include selfishness and involves treachery, deception, and a bluff. Once again, we see how deception relates to manipulation and selfishness. The process of manipulation convinces someone to do something or think in a particular way. The method of manipulation involves pressure, force, and an act of urgency. manipulation in no way relates to a polite request unless deception is involved. Deception changes the way others think. Manipulation pushes people to do something that they would not consider themselves. This shows that manipulation has a selfish purpose, as it does not satisfy the needs of the manipulated person or victim of manipulation.

People can be manipulated to do many things. They can be forced by threat or treachery to do something at their own expense. The manipulator saves money by pushing the expense to the one being manipulated. Other forms of manipulation involve creating a benefit to those creating the deceit for selfish reasons. Victims of manipulation receive no reward or benefit. The victims incur a cost either in money, time, property, convenience or emotion. Manipulation creates value or convenience to a selfish deceptive person. The victim loses in the form of some value and level of convenience.

<u>Selfishness</u>

In the bible from the book of Romans 2:8, the scripture reads: But for those who are self-seeking and do not obey the truth, but obey unrighteousness, there will be wrath and fury.

In the bible from the book of first Corinthians chapter 10 verse 24, the scripture reads: Let no one seek his own good, but the good of his neighbor.

In the bible from the book of Romans chapter 12 verse 3, the scripture reads: For by the grace given to me I say to everyone among you not to think of himself more highly than he ought to think, but to think with sober judgment, each according to the measure of faith that God has assigned.

Selfishness is the quality or condition of lacking consideration for others. People who are selfish concern themselves with their own profit or pleasure. Selfish people receive profit or pleasure at the expense of others. This is done by deception and manipulation. Again, we see how deception, manipulation, and selfishness relate to each other.

The best ways to discern selfish behavior is to identify people who carry a high ego. People who are egocentric and egotistical show self-centered behavior identified as selfish. The resulting behavior of selfishness includes being inconsiderate, thoughtless, uncaring, uncharitable, mean, greedy, and opportunistic. This behavior satisfies selfish people with ignorance to victims of selfish behavior.

Deception, Manipulation, and Selfishness

In the bible from the book of Mark chapter 7 verse 21 to 23, the scripture reads: For from within, out of the heart of man, come evil thoughts, sexual immorality, theft, murder, adultery, coveting, wickedness, deceit, sensuality, envy, slander, pride, foolishness. All these evil things come from within, and they defile a person."

In the bible from the book of 1st of John chapter 3 verse 9 says No one born of God makes a practice of sinning, for God's seed abides in him, and he cannot keep on sinning because he has been born of God.

The word evil shares a combination of attributes of deception, manipulation, and Selfishness. Deception requires manipulation and selfishness. Manipulation requires selfishness and deception. Selfishness includes deception and manipulation. All three behaviors related to each other. With the combination of all three behaviors in motion, identifying evil behavior challenges even the more astute and intuitive person.

A way to identify evil tendencies involves breaking up the behaviors of deception, manipulation, and selfishness and identifying each one. When one is identified, then the other two can be identified by relating it to the first identified behavior. For example, an act of deception identified as a behavioral flaw. This flaw in turn relates to manipulation and selfishness. Once all three behaviors show clearly that shows evil. Identifying evil involves first identifying either deception, manipulation, or selfishness. Second, the other two behaviors show relevance to the first behavior identified.

Selfish behavior requires manipulation to deceive someone. The tendency of being selfish results in deceptive manipulation. To deceive through manipulation require selfish behavior. Just know that evil behavior shares behaviors between deception, manipulation, and selfishness.

<u>Integrity</u>

A person's character is a measurement of their integrity. That character comes from a measurement of evil behavior such as deception, manipulation, and selfishness. As the bible reminds us, we are all born into sin. We have the ability to deceive, manipulate, or have selfish tendencies. We all can improve our character by keeping a watchful eye on our levels of deception, manipulation, and selfishness. By reducing all three behaviors, our integrity greatly improves and shown in our character. You language and behavior speak of your character. The ways you carry yourself and speak to others speak of your character. The more positive the character, the greater a person's integrity is. Keep check on yourself. Take a close look to see, if even to a small innocent degree, if you carry traits of deception, manipulating, or selfishness.

Behavior

Poor behaviors include hypocrisy and condemnation. Hypocrisy is the practice of claiming to have moral standards or beliefs to which one's own behavior does not conform. In other words, hypocrisy is the behavior of a person condemning others for the same behavior that they possess. It is a form of deceptive behavior previously talked about. This behavior can also be used for manipulation. Hypocrisy is for selfish purposes. This means that hypocrisy or being hypocritical falls into evil behavior. People to condemn others when they themselves should share in the condemnation use hypocrisy.

<u>Love</u>

In conclusion, just know that your language and behavior speak to your character which is a measurement of your integrity. Do you want to do better?

Look at the scriptures identified in this book and attend a bible-based Christian church. Check within yourself for characteristics of deception, manipulation, and selfishness. If you can capture those three characteristics and hold them harnessed, then you will see improved behavior. Instead, look toward LOVE, as the right behavior.

LOVE = Let Our Voice Encourage

In the bible from first Corinthians chapter 13 verses 4 to 8, it reads: Love is patient and kind; love does not envy or boast; it is not arrogant or rude. It does not insist on its own way; it is not irritable or resentful; it does not rejoice at wrongdoing but rejoices with the truth. Love bears all things, believes all things, hopes all things, endures all things. Love never ends. As for prophecies, they will pass away; as for tongues, they will cease; as for knowledge, it will pass away.

In the book of John chapter 3 verse16, it says: For God so loved the world, that he gave his only Son, that whoever believes in him should not perish but have eternal life.

From the bible, in the book of Mark chapter 12 verse 31 it says: The second is this: 'You shall love your neighbor as yourself.' There is no other commandment greater than these."

In the bible from the book of Luke chapter 6 verse 35, it says: But love your enemies, and do good, and lend, expecting nothing in return, and your reward will be great, and you will be sons of the Most High, for he is kind to the ungrateful and the evil.

David K. Ewen, M.Ed.

About the Author

About the Author: David K. Ewen, M.Ed. is an author, speaker, and publisher. He has been in the field of Education since 1988 and added on the experiences of book publishing since 1994 and has been deeply in media production, marketing, and distribution since then. As a public speaker, David K. Ewen, M.Ed. first reached the six New England states promoting the self-publishing independent press industry in 1998 while serving as Executive Director of the New England Publishers Association. This speaking tour was complimented by a weekly hour-long radio broadcast talk show hosted on WORC 1310 AM and WGFP 940 AM. The show author of the week was spun off into a short-lived weekly television show broadcasted from the CAT studios in Westborough Massachusetts. David has been deeply involved in multimedia production and distribution since 1998. David K. Ewen, M.Ed. held a second speaking tour that lasted 11 years touring the seven states of New York and New England at 52 venues lecturing on 18 different topics. This was called the "Professor Lecture Series" running from 2004 to 2015 with the flagship lecture "Publish Your Book Guaranteed" Shortly following the conclusion of the professor lecture series tour, David K. Ewen, M.Ed. went out on the global stage to speak to the nations for the purposes of training and education. As a civilian field Ambassador in education, his initial outreach was in Japan, China, Vietnam, Saudi Arabia, and Russia. David holds a faculty position at the American Academy in Beijing, China. Today, when David is working on the global stage speaking to the nations he reaches out to the civilian community in Asia, the Middle East, and Europe. The technical background of David K. Ewen, M.Ed. comes from his initial work as a quality assurance specialist and senior analyst programmer in the 1980s and 1990s. His undergraduate work at the University of Massachusetts focused on mathematics with a minor in computer science. His post-graduate focused on education with a minor in management earning him a master's degree in education in 1988 (M.Ed., Cambridge College). The business experience of David K. Ewen, M.Ed. comes from the founding of Ewen Prime Company in 1994. The experience was demonstrated during his 11-year tour in the seven states of New York and New England with the lecture, "Building and Maintaining a Profitable Consulting Practice". This was part of the "Professor Lecture Series" tour.

David K. Ewen, M.Ed.

Ambassador
Speaking to the Nations
by
David K. Ewen, M.Ed.

Silver Anniversary Series

ISBN-13: 978-1725199972

ISBN-10: 1725199971

About the Book

The book Ambassador talks about the authors role and responsibilities as a field Ambassador in the area of education. Readers will understand the personality and behaviors necessary for such a position. It is interesting to note that the international responsibility of a field Ambassador is strictly civilian in nature. This is a look at how civilians stand on the global stage and speak to the nation's as a field ambassador. The book is written in narrative form as in a lecture.